THE 44TH OF JULY

THE 44TH OF JULY

Jaswinder Bolina

OMNIDAWN PUBLISHING
OAKLAND, CALIFORNA
2019

Cover art:
"Gaurav Saraswat / EyeEm / Getty Images" (image: front cover:
Rear View Of Boy Burning Cracker During Diwali At Night)
"Merav Maroody / EyeEm / Getty Images" (image: back cover:
Fireworks display through glass window at night)

Cover typeface: Futura Std
Interior typefaces: Warnock Pro & Palatino LT Std

Cover & interior design by Cassandra Smith

Offset printed in the United States
by Sheridan Books, Chelsea, Michigan
On 55# Glatfelter B19 Antique
Acid Free Archival Quality Recycled Paper

Library of Congress Cataloging-in-Publication Data

Names: Bolina, Jaswinder, 1978- author.
Title: The 44th of July / Jaswinder Bolina.
Other titles: Forty-fourth of July
Description: Oakland, California : Omnidawn Publishing, [2019]
Identifiers: LCCN 2018040199 | ISBN 9781632430649 (pbk. : alk. paper)
Classification: LCC PS3602.O6538 A6 2019 | DDC 811/.6--dc23
LC record available at https://lccn.loc.gov/2018040199

Published by Omnidawn Publishing, Oakland, California
www.omnidawn.com (510) 237-5472 (800) 792-4957
10 9 8 7 6 5 4 3 2 1
ISBN: 978-1-63243-064-9

Robyn   Ana

&   *for*   &

Taran   Simone

However this may be, the conquest by modern man [sic] of a virgin and habitable continent was an adventure unique in human history... There can be no repetition of this until mankind [sic] lands on a planet belonging to another star.

François Bordes, "The Paleolithic in America," *The Old Stone Age*

Country, Western

Via carriage and steamer and saddle and rail,
      via twin-prop and airship and ship of the desert,
      via savannah, via steppe, via zipline and glider,
      under moat and over rampart, over barb

and under wire, over three green seas, via burro, via grapple,
      via ballistic trajectory like broke satellites cratered
      in alien dirt, like banged knuckles on the door
      of an uneasy speakeasy, we were the party after

the party nobody wanted, sober and famished, we were
      the parched fronds beggared and supplicant
      to the clouds, the clouds cool and distant
      as a bourgeoisie, and we without our sleet coats,

and we without our hail hats, with less than a shekel,
      less than a rupee, less than a kroner or any glinting
      Kennedy, three pence short of a peso, we arrived
      over guard and under sentry, via catapult, via coyote,

via many genies blinking, we arrived bats in a manse no bat
      should inhabit so we grew fin and we grew talon,
      we scrambled arachnid and jaguared in the canopy,
      dissembled, reassembled, and it's true we piss now

in marbled closets and shower indoors as if we are clergy,
      it's true no junta defiles us, no furious bomber
      or hegemon's boot, but the faces on the currency
      all watch me, the paintings in the museum say,

This is life on Earth! This is life on Earth! so I'm jealous
      of their candor, but that isn't my pasty duchess,
      that isn't my butchered messiah, that isn't my bounty
      of meat beside the gilded chalice, I'm no Medici,

and that isn't my life on earth I arrived in via wormhole,
      via subspace, via mother ship descending, in a snap-button
      sarong, in a denim sari, in my ten-gallon turban, I look
      so authentic you'd almost believe it's the 44th of July,

and I'm the sheriff of this here cow town, I'm one ace better
      than a straight flush, buzzards above the valley,
      I can see the whites of your eyes, my name is Consuela,
      you can call me *Mr. President.* You can reach for the sky.

Primary Poem

Oafish, the gods loaf, thunder-thighed,
potbellied, and fatted with answers
but fabricated of tricky WIMPs
and a few bosons only, they waddle
undetected through every collider.
No Jehovah photobombing any deep field,
no hosanna riffs the radio telescope array.
No transubstantiation in the X-ray
observatory, but here's a host
of Pringles and a half-kicked fifth
of Chablis in the Edgewater heat
of our house, cinders in the bong water,
an aspiration of quinoa in the pantry,
a belligerence of Republicans on TV
fessing how the gods prod them,
Run for Senator, Governor, or, *Run*
for President, Senator, so they run and run,
but no savior does anoint us
an exploratory committee or holy-ghost
into our inner circle or endorse you
or me for President, Faisal, our faces
by television light rendered stark
and distant as a foreign star, glitches
in the background radiation, we click
and whistle in a white noise, glint
little asterisks like twinkles from a flag pin,
our dim, lit bodies they don't believe in.

Pornograph, with Americana

Don't move to Calgary, Apna,
have sex! possibly even with me
if you're willing, not even in wedlock,
possibly backwards with one knee
on the vanity, the shower heaving
steam to the Big Band webcast
out of KCEA, Atherton, my mother
napping downstairs in the great room,
she won't know you scaled the carport,
ducked an eave with a joint and a sixer
of Stroh's, my kurta in ribbons,
your lengha undone, I put every part
of you inside my mouth and bite down
a little as if I'm a rototiller in heat,
you the agitated earth, and I love you,
honest injun! while the sun slinks
behind the Fitch's Big Boy across
the interstate, fireflies make erratic
synapses above the drainage ditches,
the fir trees sway like frat boys
at a kegger, and the neighbors
who watch us framed in the naked
window, who wish us deported
into a darker corner of the duplex,
they can clench their hymnals, Apna,
and glare, we won't go anywhere
Waheguru! Waheguru! we won't go.

Supremacy

Diodes of the cable modem haunt
the walls a watercolor now I lie awake

and listen for the grope of the king
tide tickling every jetty, for jitters

in the Nikkei Index on the other side
of night, for the boy matriculating now

into a gunman in his efficiency
apartment a couple school districts over,

the barrel bombs thumping Aleppo
while I listen, too, for the rustle

and grunt of the nationalist fitful
in the dank heat of his bedsheets,

the xenophobe fretful I'm somewhere
near, honing my chopsticks, loading

my tortas, my name writ in Gurmukhi,
he fidgets wakeful, fearful I'm awake also

reciting a scripture ruthless as his is,
and I am. I am awake and singing.

Partisan Poem

You're not the hero of this story.

You're what odor rankles
the dog into snarling, what clang

in the ductwork beggars the kid
into pleading for a nightlight

against sleep, against her dreams
of violence. You're the dread

in the cellar, the bed wetted,
what sets the adrenals leaking

their frantic mojo, what footfalls
in the alleyway force a hand

into its pocket in search of keys
to weave between the fingers.

You're what makes the fist,
what startles the breath out of me.

You spectre in the swamp gas,
you spider in a slipper, you snake

into my sleeping bag like an overcoat
pouncing from its hook in a corner

of my eye when I enter the house
in an off light, my familiar torqued

sinister, my prairie home made
alien, and you as a pupa birthed

from an acid bath in steaming
nurseries of your landing craft,

you as invading army and secret
police berating me I'm wrong

about your best intentions, and all
you ever tell me is I'm wrong

when all it ever seems to me is
the one thing worse than a good man

with a bad idea is a bad man
with a great idea, and I might be wrong,

but you are so abundant, so burdened,
so very bloated with the best ideas.

Inaugural Ball

Elsewhere,
the carpenter

must rip and strip
the pine into lumber,

must plane and miter
his planks and assemble

the tiny caskets,
the toddler-shaped

ones, must stack them
into ranks and columns

against walls
of his workshop

to the prim cadence
of an overnight World

Service anchor
on the shortwave,

must print his invoice
and deliver it

to whoever cuts
the checks, whosoever

settles the accounts
payable as the populist

spins and grins and dips
his flinching bride.

Marvel, Universe

how our hero bellows, our hero roars, blistering,
he pierces the villain's heart, his actual heart,

at the climax of a rabid ballet, slashing, hacking,
defenestrating several dozen foot soldiers en route,

these privates and lance corporals, themselves likely
conscripted men from shatter-glass inner precincts

or partisans from outer-zone midge and silo towns
with perfunctory representation in any governing

body, their best opportunity, really, to hustle, bunk,
and perish in the service of tyranny, but they agreed,

we agree, to serve, no matter how conscientious
their objections, no matter what allegiance binds

them, and these henchmen hesitate, flail,
make ready corpses as our hero quips and kisses

a once-reluctant lover to cello swells and grins
across a vista into his inevitable sequel,

while somewhere in sector 12, in a coal hill village
far from the cork-pop fireworks of liberation,

in the grayscale of surrender, someone accepts
a photograph of a lance corporal, receives a flag

and footlocker returned by the civil service
sent to inventory his cindered base, his name

registered among the lasered, among the blasted,
incinerated in the internecine interplanetary,

the expanses between cities and stars, between
empires where the expendable get expended,

but an uncle or a once-reluctant lover attends to
these relics remembering his chin dimple, his voice,

how he medaled in diving in middle school,
and one night shotgunned seven beers then scaled

the water tower to belt out the anthem of his people
under three crescent moons, and everybody fell

in love with him all at once, he didn't deserve
what the insurgents done to him, didn't owe what

liberation wanted, our duty-bound brother, the very best
of us, didn't deserve this, someone seethes beneath

the exit music, somebody glowers behind the end credits
I half-watch eating mini-pretzels in noise-canceling

headphones on an airliner thundering over the free world.

Love Song of the Assimilated

The moon's a doubloon over the bay where we live
on our houseboat. Bunny razzes I'm a busboy on account

of my black moustache, because my cowlick and color,
because my name, she knows, is Sergio Al-Ekaterinoslav,

but I say, *I'm no busboy, Bunny, I'm a yachtsman.* She says,
Somos mismos, sailor, when we're necking in the blue shade

of the blue tarp bluing the blue deck, seeming inveterate
then as market forces, unassailable there as a Federal Reserve.

Still, I tell her, I bathed as a tyke in floodplains outside Jalandhar
and stewed later in tenement flats and thought once of drinking

from a rifle. *Life frightened me, Bunny,* but now my day labors
are ended, all my water buffalo are in escrow, my laundries

automated, taxi cabs dispatched, I'm the crack proprietor
of seventy-six motels between here and Virginia.

Now I get paid, I get paid, and I get laid, which isn't alien
to the machinist, to the cocktail server or stone mason,

to the lavaplatos, dhobi wallah, or gunnery sergeant 2nd class,
but what they call a mountain in the valley, Bunny, we call a hill

on the mountain. What they call a prayer in their temple
is an algorithm in our commodities exchange.

Better a loose tycoon, I say, *than the wick in a workman's lantern.*
Better a natty cummerbund for a tool belt, our wine flutes

sweating in a tuxedo heat. Better not bother conserving
our resources for the next life. *This is the next life!* she says.

No reckoning is coming. No, only New Year's is coming
and Oscar night and Derby Day and the balloon-drop

ballyhoo of the delegate conventions I'll do up dashing
in tailored suits and pocket squares, in blazers and chinos.

I'll pass dapper as a Dixie lawyer. If anybody asks, *Where
is he from?* Bunny, tell her Baton Rouge, or say South Carolina.

If anybody asks, *Where's he* really *from?* meaning the Rangoon
Nebula, meaning the seventh moon of Guadalajara

or the ice planet Karachi, tell him I come in peace or I pledge
allegiance. Tell him, those tyrants beat their keep tonight

where widows wail in wilds where the nascent widows wail,
but I let Allah triage the bodies in his Red Crescent stations,

let Abraham play arbiter, Jesus raise the dead, I ain't a tyrant, Bunny,
I'm a citizen. That land is their land. I lie with you now

on the bay in our houseboat where I dream in English,
algorithm, algorithm, let no cussing widow wail at me.

Story in a White Diction

Then, the executive sunning poolside motions
for a margarita, a basket of chips and dip,
a detective novel or a romance novel or a novel
      about a detective romancing a suspect,

but the only English the pool girl can offer
from the lobby's lost and found is a procedural
memoir the detective writes nights staking out a bistro
      where the suspect is a sous chef, but the suspect

doesn't see her there with her notepad, her telephoto
lens, her GladWare of trail mix, and directional mic.
The suspect is eager for his shift to end so he can meet
      his Pilates instructor for a third date

on which he'll convince her, after a beet salad,
after the Wes Anderson flick, after a stroll by gaslight
through the common, he's ready for love in spite
      of the garish death of his second wife who fell

from their lofted suite onto a crystal decanter and not,
as local bloggers have suggested, the other way around.
He mutters, *She'll believe me, she'll believe me,*
      to the sine wave of the meat slicer gliding forward

and back until an entire block of prosciutto is shuffled
and stacked, his mantra so consuming he doesn't register
the executive chef's irritation at his othermindedness,
      his pestering requests to punch out early, his tats

and legal entanglements she has no patience for now
she's cutting ribbon on a third location, soon a fourth,
someday a chain, a syndicated cooking show, the cover
      of *Forbes* magazine so many middle managers

read relieving their feet of their penny loafers, grubbing
peanuts and sucking down Fiji waters, and one of them
will recognize her across the wide aisle of a Virgin America
    airliner and glance then glance again strategizing

his savvy introduction, a quipping banter, a chardonnay
segued into an exchange of private email addresses,
personal cell numbers, maybe a screw in the can,
    which is a chief ambition among men of terrible wealth

and learning, but she can do better, she thinks, slipping
on a sleep mask in her lay-flat seat en route from a TED Talk
in Palo Alto to a week's R&R in Cabo. She's on the cover
    of *Forbes* magazine for chrissakes, she can certainly

do better, she says a few days later to the pool girl
who's sweating a lot by now, her black braid plaited against
the damp back of her uniform oxford, her uniform khakis
    clutching her thighs, a sober musk overpowering

her perfume, but the executive doesn't notice any of this
when she offers, *Honey, we can all do better*, as if they're
girlfriends brunching, as if they're chitchatting in an Uber
    escaped from a crappy mixer, as if hers is a sentence

every body is serving, hers a language both of them dream in
nightly on Tempur-Pedic mattresses in adjoining row houses,
and bland ambition is the only difference between her
    and her and everybody wants to be like her.

Prepping the Exile

Concede now your ordinary
gripes, your standard evasions:
the idiots texting while snarling
your rush hour, your escapes
via back roads you best know
for a happy hour at the Gold Star,
the Black Rock, dinner, then
nightcaps at the Green Mill
till predawn raises its gray sail
in a window of the house where
you keep your things. You'll need
new things you can't even begin
to Costco, to crate or to barrel.
Forget now your kitsch and granite
kitchen, your home depots
and free peoples, the soft power
of a staycation and owning
a Roomba in the sumptuous
green of oak leaves crowning
the streetlights of your town.
This is not your town. Nobody
here woos you, no needy here
need you. The local kids beef,
their mouths a bazaar of adenoid,
slur, and molar, though you learn
their fan dances, dress yourself
in their oils and attire, articulate
a grammar that doesn't pronounce
you, their lexicon has no word
for you, but you mustn't despair.
The night is young, the snake houses
still open. Now, straighten your necktie,
professor, raise up your rickshaw,
and give us a ride.

✳✳✳

Letter to a Drone Pilot

In my dream of you perched in a turret in your blue chemise
with its white star print, my oxen move through your spyglass

trained on me in a far-off valley where my caravan trundles
into my dream of you on an overpass in your helmet

and overalls lobbing fruit at my pickup truck as I drive
between the dunes of my dream of you in a flight suit

at your high station noting every blink of my turn signal,
every dhaba I stop in for tea in my dream of you

as a thin motor whine pervading the airspace above
the fellaheen markets of my dream of you who follows me

down every arcade, into every courtyard, who listens
to my soft swallows on the phone, rifles

through my every communiqué, watches me undress
from a skylight in the thatched roof of the plaster house

of my dream of you where you sit with a panther at the foot
of your rocking chair, a hatchet on one knee, and I enter

through a beaded curtain with a bowl of dhal,
a jug of lassi for you in your headset, your dress blues,

a microphone grazing your lower lip in the monitor glow
of my dream of you, you slip your tongue into my ear,

your hand in the damp between my legs, I'm naked as the rain,
you are a banyan tree with your tangle of prop roots molesting

my entire earth in your dream of me, I tumble and flail
with a nine-pound awl and a rope saw in your dream of me

as a bull you hack your sabre through my dream of you
as an office tower and me as the zealot boy bringing you down,

darling, I do mean you harm, and you do mean me harm,
so why do you bother with restraint, dress yourself in cloud cover

as if it's a kind of habit, why quiver at your switch like a nun nearly
unwilling, as if there isn't any lust in your malice,

no feeling like a good fuck when you land your hellfire home?

Courting the Jihadi

You do the murder too easy, habibi, like an American
spewing lunatic with three rifles in a theater.

You do the murder hyperbolic, like a capitalist,
an industrialist, an imperialist razing a nation

for a salt mine. You do the murder lazy, off your soft
targets where we stand pigtailed or playing horses

in municipal districts where my cousins live,
my lovers live, strangers live who are willing

to do things for me, who bless me whenever I sneeze
in any market, any cramped plaza under clouds

that detonate slow as if they are blast plumes drowsy
with opiates, clouds that flatter whole afternoons

with that exertion, whole drenched seasons they gather
themselves up and eviscerate their bodies slow,

then go their guts go etching in the rivers and revising
the land. This is how the terrain changes.

This is how refreshment arrives, not in the plasma flash
of lightning but by the slow insistence of water.

Still, you do the murder quick like it's a bright idea,
like the cosmos is split into a faction of gods

and a faction of meat, and you're a lieutenant
for the idols, but no pulsar, no tidewater, no quark

spinning in us, not even the automatic voltage
in our ventricles pays you or me much mind

so why do you believe any god would want you
for a hammer, mammal? You're on the side

of carpal and sinew, on my side, and I can't say
I ever saw a god go, but if one of those took to our turf

demanding your head or mine, you better believe
I'd spare us both, habibi, and nail that savage to a tree.

We Bystander

we goose on the loose we mouse

in the house we fox boxed in

by hounds we stag flagging

beneath the blind we creature

in the feature we beast

into meat we phantasm

sp**k and g**k we h*ji

through the crosshairs

ni**er in the sightlines

c**t and k*ke we

r*ghead the collateral

we the p*lice-beat placards

in the graveyard we what

the dr*nes drop ticks

in the kill list the st*tesm*n count

and the g*nm*n counter

the dem*g*gues thump

and the h*ly m*n thunder

duck duck bang tocks the fuse

in the fanny pack duck duck

bang barks the muzzle

of the c*rbine duck duck bang

breaks the story in the n*wscast

we watch we wait scraps

in the g*me pl*n we plucked

we dropped duck duck bang

Rubble Causeway, Rubble Clinic

Shatter temple, splinter soup kitchen, incarcerate
    the beat reporters and abolish the council, desecrate
    the mosque and dispatch the mayor, you can't delete
    the city. The people are still there shielding their tweens

on buses with their grilles kicked in, the tweens are still there
    blinking at you, every bell there still, and desolate
    the skate park, desolate the market, desolate our
    CorningWare crusted con chutney, avec sofrito and fish

sauce stagnant in the washbasins, you can cleanse the ethnics,
    expel every interloper, and cordon the border, but you can't
    scrub the city, its pipework of phlegm, its hair knot
    of telecom cables, subway rave of rats and the last of us

sheltering underground, though come, all you autocrats coiffed,
    you silken thugs, come, all you hard men in loafers,
    root out the last of us, leave her body for the crows,
    but the morgue is still there with its bone show.

Everywhere our graffiti sings. Chlorinate the hood
    and napalm the precinct, you can't incinerate the city,
    our mercury stashed in your groundwater, dioxides
    stowed in your jet stream, the crust and mantle

remember you can't eradicate the city, our broadcasts already
    transmitted, they radio our swelter into the cosmos
    so the cosmos remembers our traffic and weather together,
    news on the hour, sports on the 4s, the pitchmen pimping

0% down on all living and dining room furniture, and the living
     remember dining, furniture, napping in flats to the shush
     of tires, billow of limbs, tangle of curtains, somehow
     a siren always receding, somehow the baby still breathing.

Epistemic Love Poem

If there were a verb meaning 'to believe falsely', it would not have any
significant first-person present indicative.

Ludwig Wittgenstein, *Philosophical Investigations*

In Crimea now the larks might be muzzled by artillery
and crap weather, how should I know? In Haifa now
the guns must be running, I have no idea. In Kobani,
a boy is waxing a Kalashnikov, a boy is waning
in a blood puddle, I don't know. I'm not in Missouri.
I'm not in Humboldt Park or Harlem. I'm here with you,
wrought simple and plain happy. The only city I know
is your city, is your city block, your boulevard between
the German bar and the orthodontist's. The only city
I know is the square of sidewalk your shadow paints.
Everywhere else is switched off now, every current
stilled, the Gulf Stream is in sleep mode, its porpoises
unplugged, its seagulls powered down dangling
from clouds that are stuck static in their full upright
and locked positions. No carbon is there baking
the human sky, no typhoon, no Ebola churning.
No Donald Trump is there in his white office, no
Mitch McConnell in the garret of his own braincase,
no pope infallible, no lama enlightened, no ayatollah
knows what I know now I know you, and no, I don't
call you *darling*. I don't call you *honey* or *sugar* or *babe*,
those names made for other bodies, those noises lamed
by other people, and the other bodies are switched off
slack mannequins on trolley cars, in Hondas, in jets
stopped over Crimea, over Kobani and Haifa, everyone
dumbstruck everywhere still as a book on a shelf.
If it isn't written by you, I won't read it. If it isn't about you,
I won't own it. I won't call you *bunny* or *sweetheart*
or *pumpkin* now I know you are my wild earthquake,
my ontological kazoo, my dizzy robin of ghost feathers,

your voice is a brontosaur. It's bigger than everything.
Your mind is bigger than mine, it frightens me,
but I kiss your shins and shoulders now, I kiss your hips,
it's like kissing rainwater, though I know no rain
exists if it isn't kissing your face. I'm being ridiculous,
I know! But, my chest is a rowboat rolled over and over,
my chest is a boulder, the boulder crashed through
the floodlight of my chest, and I believe falsely now
no horror exists. I believe falsely no other joy exists.
I believe in every love song now every love song
is wrong that doesn't know you, my transcendental
tea cup, my butter knife in a light socket, you are
my space plane, my only space plane, I do dare
to eat a peach, I do dare disturb the universe,
and if the universe turns out to be a false front,
if the universe is a figment in a dog's eye or the dog
brain of some other universe, I don't need to know
now I know you I don't know I don't need to know.

Texting the Beloved

Hark! the ghetto lark puffs out
a ditty in the cucumber glow

of the BP filling station sign tonight I should be in Taipei
with you I'm not in Taipei but isn't it easier to adore you

for the fact you aren't around like a bumper crop prefigured
in a blank field by the idle farmhand in winter alone

who is me wheeling my Chevy through this and every
adjacent county you aren't resident in when you're landed

at Pudong at Orly are in a railcar of the TGV these messages
you send I read and read again as if the letters made better

than a dumb phonics as if the slim brick of Gorilla Glass®
in the cupholder could make the vapor your mouth makes

the way a beached conch makes the rush of the sea
which is a myth and bad analogy but when I reply

you become the Aegean I sink my sheet music into
these notes I send jingle and twitch in your shirt pocket

or better your pants pocket! whatever time zone country
code you dwell in my dispatches ping into your hushed couchette

your quiet museo and distant kabuki its audience lit up
so sudden they hiss like flares sprung over the countryside

I traverse now knowing what the flare knows its only effort is
in arresting some attention these thumb-punched confessions

I transmit to you in Beirut in Khartoum or in San Sebastian
I should pull over to type them but I don't pull over I go faster

past radar gun and dashboard cam past local law
and local trooper beneath those sexless analysts

at the NSA who sit awake all night intercepting your reply
my love they couldn't possibly apprehend it

The Wedding Poem

Is it your fallout shelter? Is it your diesel generator?
Is it the truth in your pamphlets, your incontrovertible

alien and undeniable sasquatch? Is it your stockpile
of Spam and ammo or the campfire's gleam crinkled

in the dome of your aluminum hat that so beguiles me?
Woe, those Saskatchewan nights I huddled without you,

my camera on a hair trigger, my motion sensors tensing.
I listened for your ghost dogs baying in the hollows,

for your poltergeist banging in my barn loft.
I waited for your landing lights igniting my tree line,

for your tractor beam to abduct, dissect, and erase me.
Those years alone with my Ouija board, I pleaded

for you to hijack my airwaves, to come invade
my Winnebago, come bodysnatch me! I demanded

a simple proof of you, your puff of smoke drifted
over my grassy knoll, your Freemasons peeking

into my Bohemian Grove, but the specter of you,
I couldn't capture, so no one believed me. Your signals

in the noise, I couldn't decipher, and no one believed me.
Nobody ever believed me until you believed me.

Now, my skull and bones inducted into the conspiracy
of your company, your Opus Dei inviting my Illuminati,

now you are real so I am real, now shudders the zombie
night, the end is nigh, only you believe me. Now, divvy up

the jerky, my heart. Ration out the trail mix, my one and only.
I'll bolt the cellar door, you load the crossbows,

I have no idea what happens next!

New Adventures in Sci-fi

We inhabit a bland planet, prattle and shop in precincts
no photons torpedo. Nobody wormholes, nobody

telekinetic. Not one of us can fly, but we don't sweat
the interest accruing on our MasterCards either.

No caps on our data plans, no gaps in our Medicaid
through the fevers of spring, through our seventeen

months of summer, our seven throngs of fall
when the leaves change several times an hour

until it snows those days we really need it to snow
so the sun can thaw the barrio dry, lay itself easy

as a leg draped across your legs on a porch swing.
Everybody has a porch swing the beat cops wave to

when they pass. They don't protect us bloody.
They don't police the teeth out of our heads

or thump us as if they are monsters afraid
of the dark. We aren't fearful of any invaders

emigrating into our Oort cloud. No jingo caucus
gums up our galactic congress. No bigot polemic

commandeers our election cycle. Our super PACs
protect us, our lobbyists defend us, even

our Republicans consider our expertise.
Not one is an American. There's no such thing

as Americans. There are only bisexuals,
all forty-six of our black presidents, all thirty-seven

of them women, all of us infatuated
with each other, and all our caliphs desire

is a pride parade. All our Zions require mutual
consent there is no God, and there is no God

so we get on with our hydroponics and barbecue
so when the aliens come, they come for our cuisine.

They stay for our bar scene, tip us heavy,
split their spliffs with us at sunup on the beach

before breakfast, before taking us for a matinee
where they marvel at our CGI, the RealD 3D

of our angst that depicts them wicked as we are,
hungry grunts always fixing for a fight.

The Bar Poem

And if it turns out Lahore is at the proximate
center of a cloud-shaped multiverse, every universe
a droplet, every moth in Punjab the mortal flicker
of an otherlife; if there's an otherlife, this trig
and nova show just a third or thirty-third expansion
of a boundless quantum mud, and there aren't any
mountain spirits, no papacy or patron saints logging
our masturbations, you mulling boneheaded
sermons in erroneous temples, me resting
on the wrong day, pleading at an incoherent altar,
and if the space gurus arrive curing unemployment
and angst, if they confirm the definitive merits
of deregulation but also the indispensable covenant
of a social safety net, if they affirm Otis Redding
is better than the Beatles or the Stones, Bach pedantic,
Lata Mangeshkar more intricate than Ovid,
and of course *Anne of Green Gables* over *Harry Potter*,
of course Michael over LeBron, of course Serena,
and yes, the milk past its sell-by date is fine,
and no, you don't look fat in those pants,
but the gecko tat and tongue stud in '98
were a bad idea, but there's no such thing as '98,
and you were wrong about Tupac, right about
kumquats, wrong about Nietzsche, and if the unearthly
Übermenschen arrive in their Jesus-shaped starship
to say they've been watching us a long time,
that we are critical as paperclips, redeemable
but nearer to the apes than the angels, will you finally
put your beer down, Bernardo, settle your tab,
and walk the brief, hushed blocks home?

In Memory of My Vices

I miss the idiocy, I miss the glee,
the radiator clang of the dim

apartments. Cozy the joint circles
of winter dilating into the bonfires

of spring, a whiskey handle tipped
and dipping from face to face to face,

a carousel, somebody always doubled
over whooping on the screen porch,

somebody caressing someone beneath
a poker table. Maybe it was me,

maybe you downing boilermakers
enough so everybody sounded

like a poem by e.e. cummings,
us shrooming till the moon looked

globular, bulged low and umber,
a spaceport above snakeskin kinks

of the river trail slinking into a riot
of pines. We fretted an ordinary

death then, by late shift, by loan debt
and subdivision so you leapt tipsy

as a depth charge into dark water.
I made like a rocket and chased

my satellite head. You were a tailpipe,
I was a sunburn smoking without thinking

of carcinomas. *Did you ever think about*
a carcinoma? you'd ask, bolting

up from the little barcode of coke
on the dash. *Sure, but like a bad verdict*

might get overturned on appeal,
which was the worst I imagined

would happen to us heady gentry
of the North Woods driving back

to hipster districts, no harm, no foul,
no police ever made us bleed.

Ekphrastic Poem

To the owners of Brâncuşis, of box seats
and equity, of assorted rare charcuterie,
you owners of Rothkos, Riviera flats,
and lullabies of port, of derivatives,
de Koonings, of tailors, decorators,
and sommeliers, you owners of the want
for a sommelier: I never do cellar much
Yellowtail in my Frigidaire. I pick it quick
at the Walgreens, down it with a jar of olives,
a brick of cheddar on the fire escape afternoons
your options are vesting, your markets
combusting, your huddled assets yearning
to spree free, you owners of Pradas, Teslas,
of a Calder and a major minor canvas
by Jasper Johns, here's my shtick
and my portfolio. I'm an artist also,
horn-rimmed, buzz-cut, a real Marxist,
honest to God. Here's my portrait of a boy
in a blue frock with a Glock among bluebells,
here my mosaics of steam, my triptychs
of beef, a mixed media panel of a bridge
in Brooklyn I'd like to sell you. I'm not really
a Marxist. I'm a Master of Fine Arts, honest.
I want a Tesla too, a mahogany office, a brokerage,
and tenure. I earned it. You have no idea
how hungry I earned it those years momma
was as an arc welder, daddy worked secretary,
and neither gave a damn about my art, honest,
the only thing those mopes ever covered
was the rent, the electric, tuition, and gas.

What We Call a Mountain in the Valley, They Call a Hill on the Mountain

Aren't the rigors of traffic ample? Aren't child-rearing
      and the triumph of income over expenditure ambition
enough? Aren't your hours already glutted with language

      and image, with pundit and selfie? Why do you fidget
over your poem when ten minutes in a conjugal visit trailer
      would be a venture more fruitful, a project more tactile

and lucid? Can you conjure a love that substantial, a lyric more
      American than the one in the bed of the penitentiary
nestled between soybean fields? Would you be a witness vigilant

      as the guard in a tower there? Are your visions exacting
as the sniper's, your anxieties urgent as the fugitive's,
      your art subversive as the coyote's smuggling

the escaped, run-ragged, in tunnels to Albuquerque,
      in boatloads to Palermo, in pickup trucks from Aleppo?
Can you manufacture a longing so hollow, a sorrow gnawing

      dogged as the refugee's when she's cuffed by the border
patrol? Is your desire more ferocious than the insurgent's
      on the lam, your subject more global

than the drone's that stalks him? Is your aesthetic piercing
      as the infrared of its targeting scope, your epiphanies
drastic as the bride's when her wedding is detonated in error,

your regret so indelible, your angst so ineffable
as the corporal's in his Humvee deployed to catalog
        the corpses in their eveningwear? And if it is,

you'd offer us what? A quatrain scolding the combatants?
        A stanza bronzing the incidental dead? Will your poem
be inventive as an IED, candid as a suicide vest?

        Will it be twelve poems? Is it even in prose?
And when the corporal is discharged into his tenement home
        where schoolboys are perforated by their neighbors,

pedestrians billy-clubbed, tasered, and shot dead by the law,
        you think there's a poetry for that? That you'll write it
concrete and specific? Will you write what you know?

        Will you call it "Hip Hop Sweatshop"
or "Of the Different Progress of Opulence in Different Nations"
        or "Lying in a Hammock at William Duffy's Farm

in Pine Island, Minnesota, Part Two"? Will you write it
        on a MacBook? Will you write it in a Starbucks?
Will it tell us, *You have wasted your life?* It'll tell us what you know

        and don't know and more than we know?
And if we don't comprehend it, do you believe someday we will?
        That the poem will blossom before us some morning

like a green light at Daytona? Like a moonshot
        over the bleachers? It'll be earnest as bourbon,
pervasive as coal coke, final as ash in the urn? Will it loom

granite and complicated, lauding and mournful
as a monument on The National Mall? And in the clarity
of its aftermath, do you think we'll call on you?

We'll call on you to ride out of your garret on a bull
with your flower? Are you awaiting our signal?
If it resembles indifference, don't misunderstand us.

We're working a double. We're stuck on the line
or jammed up in traffic or running for cover,
ducking the shift boss, the loan officer, parole

officer, the incoming ordnance, hoping for home
by seven to coax a forkful of spinach into the kid
and the kid into bed. We could use a ceasefire.

We could use a sick day and a debt holiday,
an airlift or an aid worker, an attorney and some UN
intervention, but as soon as the police

withdraw to their barracks, soon as the militants retire
to their prayers, the banker finishes foreclosing,
and the oncologist completes her brutal portrait,

soon as the check clears, and the gun clips
empty their daily refrain, then, poet, then
come give us your tortured song.

Caterpillar

When I'm waiting in the examination room
of the dermatology clinic for Dr. Fine to arrive
and undo the six stitches knitted into my jawline,
it's superfluous to ruminate on beauty
and the marvelous human machine. The city
doesn't need another treatise on healing,
another ode to pulchritude. It needs more lidocaine,
compression wraps, 0.9% bacteriostatic solution,
and more diamond-edged cutting blades
for the road workers incising Halsted Street
four stories below the window, more gauzy
cirrus bandaging the jawbreaker-blue dome
of afternoon, more of the scaffolding that gives
the skyline the appearance of a patient in traction
so the whole of Chicago feels always
unfinished. Beauty is too easy. The serene
brown bottle and its white block font plainly
stating ALCOHOL is beautiful for its honesty,
and the glittery diode in the catastrophic red
of a fire alarm on the wall is beautiful in its pent-up
vigilance, and the cover of *People* magazine there
on the rack is flat-out ravishing with its full-bleed
photographs, its brash pronouncements. It says
ELIN NORDEGREN IS DATING AGAIN.
What a relief! Elin Nordegren is too gorgeous
to go it alone, and though I'm uncertain who she is
or on what reef she's been lacerated after what
wreckage of marriage to emerge again into romance
as if a deity arisen out of the sea, I'm concerned
for her wellbeing same as the motorists who move
to the curb to permit the anonymous, wailing
ambulance to pass, a gesture that serves as proof
humble acts of astonishing beauty are possible
even in the rancor of traffic. And it's true Dr. Fine,
first name Lauren, exudes a confidence that begets

elegance which begets grace so she's awful beautiful
too, more so than Elin Nordegren, and more so
for the ring on her finger which makes her utterly
unavailable for dating, but I await her still
on the butcher paper of the exam bed with sutures
in my face that give me the appearance of being
more rugged and vulnerable than I am, more beautiful
and true, though honestly I've had my fill of beauty
and truth. I need to know the uncertain and the scarred also
so I don't mistake this for a place I'm welcome to linger in
forever expecting an exquisite other to enter and mend me.
    No, don't dally any longer. Open the door,
    doctor, and deliver your terrible news.

The Tallest Building in America

2011

In the season of her first cancer, my sister looms over

lamp posts, broadcast antennas, over cicadas in flight.
News helicopters chuckle below her, and I can see her

from every corner druggist. I can see her from the pier
at Pratt Street Beach, from the botanic gardens in Glencoe,

from every expressway and ring road. I can see her from Ohio.
Or, maybe it's her tumor, yes, her tumor is the tallest

building in America rising into her chest like a spire shoved
into the troposphere. I call it her first cancer because any cancer

that isn't the last cancer is an only fleetingly crowned behemoth
crowding her skyline. Any new cancer will be much, much taller,

so the next cancer becomes the tallest building in America.
Every road goes there. When I think this way of the epic,

encroaching future, I become the tallest building in America
able to see over quivering horizons. The President

must feel this too when our civic maladies metastasize
into national disasters, and when he does, he's the tallest

building in America until his agenda is thwarted
by the Majority Whip so the Speaker of the House is certain

he's the tallest building in America, but the Fox Newsroom
overlooking The Avenue of the Americas is taller.

For years, the kitschy white folks who yammer there tell me
Osama bin Laden is the tallest building in America,

and it's best to throw boots through his windows until
the weather gets in, until his rebar corrodes, until he teeters

into the sea. When this happens, the headquarters
of the Central Intelligence Agency in Langley, Virginia,

becomes the tallest building in America, though the Chamber
of Commerce is much, much taller. It worries China is rising

monstrous and tall, but I remember when stern Russia
lumbered larger, and I'm nostalgic then for our antique enemies.

Nostalgia always has been the tallest building in America,
but later I'm walking through the elastic shadows

of Fullerton Avenue to the Lincoln Park Zoo to wonder
at the hopeless, daffy giraffes, or I'm in the Signature Room

of the Hancock Building for a bourbon alone, and I think, No,
above all of these, my sister is the tallest building in America.

But, all her joists are showing. Scaffoldings hem her.
Work lights scream from floor-to-ceiling gaps in her

where windows should go, but there aren't any windows
so the monsoons of autumn roil clear through,

and from this height the other buildings are small, the people
beneath them smaller, their other concerns minute,

their other catastrophes even smaller, those other folks remote
little lymph nodes about their diligent business, their other lives

enduring in a sanguine nation, in a small and temporary country.

Sélection de Vin de Proprietaires

Your cheekbones jut polar-hued in the daemon light

    of a smartphone screen into which you tap home
    your version of Paris as if it's a fact: synaptic

shimmer of moon on the river, gaslights of the certain
café, the stop-motion theatric of so many perched Rodins,

but in a story about Paris, you shouldn't bother with these
or with pigeons and the cathedral, with hatchbacks

    and hatchbacks and scooters on a Rue, with the hours agog
    in the Pompidou supplicant beneath all of that barking art.

In a story about Paris, you shouldn't mention Paris

    which is an idea baroque and embellished as God.
    Of course the street names are hummed ditties,

the crosswalks are keys of a courtly piano, and you order
a Côtes du Rhône as if there's a metaphysic in it then trill

a *merci* to the server as if all gratitude is music,
all music gratitude, which it probably is, but

    I still haven't figured how everyone here wears a scarf
    in the kitchen heat of summer, how they all smoke,

and nobody runs, and if they do we never see anybody panting.

    Don't they have interest payments? Have they no finicky
    circuit or jittery transistor? Do their supply lines never

corrode, their bodies never go to Les Centres de Santé to ride
gurneys like black taxis from the Pont Oncologie to the Place

Radiologie where the image of the brain meat is like a petal
on a black bough and all of that but also a slop of arteries

and gutters and zones so the pulp of the mind emerges
as if it's a city we visit on holiday from a more native state,

a more permanent occupation, the self as a tourist fiction?

I suppose they must, but you wouldn't know by looking
at them, which is what makes me feel so foreign

and gloomy and in Paris no less! which is better than Boise or flat
Tampa, and I'm with you! even your thumbs are exuberant

as the fizz in a Vichy water, the plum sex of your scarf,
your swift cigarette in this 61st minute of a 25th hour,

the pigeons are fat oboes, the cathedral thinks it's a dove,
and I'd almost believe my name is Elise, yours is Henri,

and we live here, my liege, easy as lilies in a boneyard.

Station

On a sunny day, you understand why people say, "If Heaven isn't what it's cracked up to be, send me back to Gimmelwald."

Rick Steves, "Switzerland's Jungfrau Region: Best of the Alps,"
Rick Steves' Europe

Send me back, Heaven, send me back
to alphorn, wiener, unknowing,
and schnitzel. Send me back
to dopplebock, uncertainty,
the mountains, and the Mountain
Hostel. I miss the rumpled earth.
I miss the 90s. Send me back,
send me back to Gimmelwald,
to my pack and flask, my abandon,
map, and Eurail pass, to sweating
the too little left in my earthly
accounts and the sky blue
box of Camels I smoked
unrepentant on a sunny day
awaiting a train to Interlaken
to Prague to a profound lust
or a petty love maybe and flaming
absinthes in the lung-cut
of Slavic winter. Un-punch
my loyalty card and, Heaven,
release me from the quid pro quo
of devotion, my humility exchanged
for your cache of dead pets and relatives
chitchatting at an unrelenting buffet,
my chastity for your answer key,
and expel me into the dizzy of morning,
1999, the fidget of waiting for a train,
what wonders in the goddamned
Gimmelwald of my good brain.

Second Variation on a Theme by César Vallejo

I'll die in Chicago on a Tuesday, midsentence
on a muggy evening, my entreaties unfinished,
I'll die demented and murmuring asleep in my bed.
I'll wither in a ward in Chicago and die of woe

as if an infantry in 1914 or like a codger of pestilence
in the 14th century. I'll die irradiated and eradicated
in Coral Gables in 2076. I'll die everywhere and for all
time like a loosed balloon or blunt as a beer bottle

dropped from a fire escape. I'll die in Chicago
on a muggy evening lousy with estate planners
and anesthetists in a week punctuated by serial blips

of a renal pump. I'll die quiet in Chicago,
what a drag it will be, how feckless and feeble
it will be to die on a Tuesday amid the zoom zoom

of weed whackers, the unending industry
of the trash collectors, buzz in the fuse boxes,
not furious as a Hoover in a stairwell or regal
as a bugle on a 747 but meek as the reggae whine

bleeding from the earbuds plugged into the head
next to mine on the 22 bus. What a humdrum thing
it'll be on a Tuesday in Chicago in which I lope
into the long spike of death and become simple

as the bodies this morning in Homs and in Hamah,
in Damascus and Deraa. I'll die on a Tuesday like today
is a Tuesday, and I'll die in Chicago in 1978 and in Paris

in 1938 and in Damascus in 2013. I'll die everywhere
and for all time as when a body is lashed and is shelled,
as when a body is punctured this morning in Idlib,

its torn animal interior, its machines un-machining,
it dies in Chicago too. No soul chatters eternal.
Protein mishmash and cortical noise, the soul trembles
on dirt among despots. A rifle butt can end it.

But, the bones of my arms are fixed today
in their good sockets. My soul is wired by dendrites
into its power supply. All my exiles and all the roads
are ahead of me so I rouse myself in the democratic vista

to launder my sheets and hit up the Kroger
for yogurt and bread. I empty the dustbins
and Tuesdays forget my trash at the curb.

I sit at the plasma hearth of the television set,
an ancient at a tribal fire in his brute regime,
and I'll die this way in the confederacy of Tuesdays

and Thursdays, the sweeps weeks and no-term
annual contracts, unlimited nights and weekends
in the mundane practice of life, dull rot of the flesh,
on a Tuesday in which Jaswinder Bolina is dead

as the dead in Deraa, their lipids combusting too
on Dearborn Avenue, their dendrites disconnecting,

slick tesserae on the façades of Chicago, their ulnas
on State Street, humeri dead wet and steaming on 95th

  on a Tuesday so like a Tuesday in which Jaswinder
Bolina is dead. Molotov his palace, fell every monument,
and rechristen the roads on a Tuesday in which

  Jaswinder Bolina is dead and Bashar al-Assad is dead
and Vladimir Putin is dead. Xi Jinping is dead,
and the eye sockets of every dead executive are lidded

  with half dollars, and Shimon Peres is dead,
and Ban Ki-moon is dead, and Barack Obama is dead
as Jaswinder Bolina is dead as every dead idol, every prophet,
Ibrahim and Isa dead, Muhammad dead,

  and the dead bells stilled in their dead steeples,
the dead minarets emptied of dead muezzins,
now sing, all you daughters of Deraa,
if it please you to sing.

Guernica

None of it is ghastly. Not the hot nickel in the earhole,
not the molars on the awning, not the shrapnel in the nieces.
Waziristan is a ripped meniscus, Yemen is a slit tendon,

Peshawar is a cut eye, and Boston is a plunked batsman.
Look at its broke nose. Look at its plum contusion.
A cow town on a cow path on the crooked coast

of a cowed country, look at it rocked and fuming in a mimic
of Gaza, a spit image of Tel Aviv. None of it is ghastly.
Not the bone meal in the poppy field, not the plastique

in the pressure cooker, not the ball bearings in the corpses
or the robots in the clouds. Go, you drone turret gunners,
it isn't the ordnance erupting in the bystander but your distance

from her that's ghastly. Go you keen jihadi, it isn't the bone-
wet massacre, but your deliberate imprecisions are ghastly.
Homicidal the bureaucrats, genocidal the martyrs,

immolate your own Toyotas, not me in my Fiat.
I only want to flirt with the bartender. She's a Pisces.
Her name is Judy. She speaks seven languages.

I forget how to spell mahjong when she whispers
mahjonnngg in the beer light. I forget my address.
I would give her four roses. I would cook her paella.

I'd invite her to Guernica. The whole city is a gravestone,
su nombre es sinónimo de *muerte* en todas las lenguas,
but it's near to the sea and the hills, the hills, the hills.

Lipid and sinew in the alluvium, I'd walk the fatted earth
giddy with Judy in Guernica where carnage is a fact,
so it isn't the facts, but how I become accustomed to them

that's ghastly. Here are four roses. Here's a bowl of paella.
It's the fifteenth of April. It's the sixth of August
and the fourteenth of February. It's the eleventh of September,

Judy, we live now in Guernica. Let's buy insurance.
Let's start a 401k. Let's make a baby and name her *Fallujah*.
Name her *Mumbai* which is Hindi for *Boston* which is English

for *Kabul*. Let's name her *New York City*. Daughter, I know not
who you'll slaughter or why, but do the killing at least
with the meat of your own good hands.

Self-portrait as a Gene Sequence

If this transmission should find you continents removed
from my last confirmed location, in your era of no-go

glaciers where your people tinder the jungle and marsh-make
their tundra, and you're reading this there on your screen porch

in the Tropic of Glasgow where you awoke this morning
to what seemed at first a loon beneath your pillow

but turned out to be an errant tsunami siren looning through an
open window from a tranquil valley nearer the coast—

if you have on a sundress in curl-kinking humidity,
in dense air greasing your brown skin while puffed sails bob

like dunce caps on a firth beneath contrails of space planes
too distant to hear while children ricochet around your yard

in polymer rompers when the youngest, the big-nosed,
sentimental one with a freckle on his right nostril, with a hint

of a lisp and a penchant for ketchup on his crackers,
stops his slug hunt in the garden to peer at the city centre

in the lowlands through kilometres of smog—if he interrupts
your bagel and reading to ask what the cranes down there

are building or how the cranes are built—if he asks
about the inception of metallurgy or the invention of glass—

Why is there brick, steel, and siding? Why is there duct tape
instead of nothing?—as you're reading this there in that nation

World Cups and World Cups hence and you find yourself
uncertain of how to begin, hand him your hammer. Show him

his elbow should make like a lever, his wrist a hinge.
Tell him to mix his water into concrete, not the concrete

into water. He should stagger his blockwork and toe-nail
his jack studs. You should soap-test his gas lines, pressure-test

his valves, trip every circuit before he messes
with any electric, then explain how the builders are lesser

than the building, the toolmakers lesser than the tools.
No one will look on his works and despair, but he might

make time-and-a-half evenings and weekends.
He might manage vision and dental and retire with a pension.

Certainly, he'll drink too much, but all that will come later.
Now, smooth the cowlick jutting from the cyclone of hair

at the crown of his head like humans do. Don't mention
the rest of us punched silent rivets in his cell walls, us proteins

that rebar his brickface, that buttress his animal architecture,
now warm, now capable, now built of the junkyard dead.

Washington B.C.

Before capitol, before capital, before cash or crony, elector
  or college, before car alarms crooning through the bleak
  constituencies of night before a continental breakfast
  or a Continental Congress, before commerce,

before currency, before candidate and caucus, city or census,
  before any colonial come converting with his convoys
  of stink, of smallpox and famine, before Conservative,
  before Christian, before 501(c)(4) and Colt .45,

before a single Carolina, before cotton, before collar and shackle,
  before Caucasian, before Colored Only, before cavalry
  and cannon, before Custer, MacArthur, or any alabaster
  chessmen charting the compact geometries of war,

before you corner, accost, and attack me, call me a camel fucker
  in traffic for what color the light makes of my skin coat,
  before I can counter, you drive off in your Jeep Grand
  Cherokee to your corner of the cellular coverage map,

but before you crack open a cold can of Coors with your bucket
  of chicken, your Diet Coke with a casserole or Lean Cuisine,
  before your nightly quarrel with the newscast, before couch
  or Comcast, before you can cuss, before you can speak,

before you could crawl, before your granddaddy's granddaddy
  put cock into conquest before Conestoga, before Columbus,
  before Carthage or Celt, before clockwork and calculus,
  of course before Christ, a century of centuries before any fable

of Christ, before country, before colony, before church or state,
  there are mastodons in the hollers, egret eggs in the marshes,
  maize enough for sixty thousand seasons, and a boy culling
  oysters there from his brisk Chesepiooc before chemical,

before contaminant, before English and alphabet, in the bounty
  of your absence, other gods walk upon his water,
  in the empires of your nonexistence, other predators
  circle his firelight, lick vicious, efficient and indifferent,

they strike.

Grateful acknowledgment to editors of the following journals in which versions of these poems previously appeared:

At Length	What We Call a Mountain in the Valley, They Call a Hill on the Mountain
BOMBlog	Caterpillar
Connotation Press	Guernica
Colorado Review	Story In a White Diction
	Courting the Jihadi
Copper Nickel	Epistemic Love Poem
	The Wedding Poem
Electric Literature	Station
Fanzine	Sélection de Vin de Proprietaires
	Country Western
Guernica	Love Song of the Assimilated
Interim	Primary Poem (under the title "Political Poem")
	In Memory of My Vices
The Miami Rail	Supremacy
OmniVerse	Pornograph, with Americana
	We Bystander
	Ekphrastic Poem
Pleiades	The Tallest Building in America
Pinwheel	Inaugural Ball
	Rubble Causeway, Rubble Clinic
The Rumpus	Partisan Poem
	Washington B.C.
Seneca Review	The Bar Poem
	Prepping the Exile
Southeast Review	Second Variation on a Theme by César Vallejo
The Volta	New Adventures in Sci-fi
Witness	Letter to a Drone Pilot
	Self-Portrait as a Gene Sequence
	Texting the Beloved

Several of these poems appeared in earlier draft in the digital chapbook *The Tallest Building in America* from Floating Wolf Quarterly. Many thanks to editor Christopher Louvet for publishing that collection.

Jaswinder Bolina was born in Chicago in 1978. He is author
of *Phantom Camera* (2013), *Carrier Wave* (2006), and the digital
chapbook *The Tallest Building in America* (2014). His poems and
essays have appeared widely in the U.S. and abroad and have
been included in several anthologies including *The Best American
Poetry* and *The Norton Reader*. He teaches on the faculty of the
MFA Program in Creative Writing at the University of Miami.

The 44th of July
by Jaswinder Bolina

Cover art:
"Gaurav Saraswat / EyeEm / Getty Images" (image: front cover:
Rear View Of Boy Burning Cracker During Diwali At Night)
"Merav Maroody / EyeEm / Getty Images" (image: back cover:
Fireworks display through glass window at night)
Cover typeface: Futura Std
Interior typefaces: Warnock Pro & Palatino LT Std

Cover & interior design by Cassandra Smith

Offset printed in the United States
by Sheridan Books, Chelsea, Michigan
On 55# Glatfelter B19 Antique
Acid Free Archival Quality Recycled Paper

Publication of this book was made possible in part by gifts from:
Mary Mackey
Francesca Bell
Katherine & John Gravendyk, in honor of Hillary Gravendyk
The New Place Fund

Omnidawn Publishing
Oakland, California
Staff and Volunteers, 2018–2019
Rusty Morrison & Ken Keegan, senior editors & co-publishers
Gillian Olivia Blythe Hamel, senior poetry editor & editor, OmniVerse
Trisha Peck, managing editor & program director
Cassandra Smith, poetry editor & book designer
Sharon Zetter, poetry editor and book designer
Liza Flum, poetry editor
Avren Keating, poetry editor & fiction editor
Juliana Paslay, fiction editor
Gail Aronson, fiction editor
SD Sumner, copyeditor
Emily Alexander, marketing manager
Lucy Burns, marketing assistant
Anna Morrison, marketing and editorial assistant
Terry A. Taplin, marketing assistant, social media
Caeden Dudley, editorial production assistant
Hiba Mohammadi, marketing assistant